LET'S PLAY
Basketball

Karen Durrie

MEDIA ENHANCED BOOKS

AV2 BY WEIGL™

ADDED VALUE • AUDIO VISUAL

Go to **www.av2books.com,** and enter this book's unique code.

BOOK CODE

F420738

AV2 by Weigl brings you media enhanced books that support active learning.

AV² provides enriched content that supplements and complements this book. Weigl's AV² books strive to create inspired learning and engage young minds in a total learning experience.

Your AV² Media Enhanced books come alive with...

Audio
Listen to sections of the book read aloud.

Video
Watch informative video clips.

Embedded Weblinks
Gain additional information for research.

Try This!
Complete activities and hands-on experiments.

Key Words
Study vocabulary, and complete a matching word activity.

Quizzes
Test your knowledge.

Slide Show
View images and captions, and prepare a presentation.

... and much, much more!

Published by AV² by Weigl
350 5th Avenue, 59th Floor New York, NY 10118
Website: www.av2books.com   www.weigl.com

Durrie, Karen.
 Basketball / Karen Durrie.
   p. cm. -- (Let's play)
 ISBN 978-1-61690-938-3 (hardcover : alk. paper) -- ISBN 978-1-61690-584-2 (online)
 1. Basketball--Juvenile literature. I. Title.
 GV885.1.D87 2011
 796.323--dc23
                              2011023429

Printed in the United States of America in North Mankato, Minnesota
1 2 3 4 5 6 7 8 9 0 15 14 13 12 11

062011
WEP030611

Project Coordinator: Karen Durrie Art Director: Terry Paulhus

Weigl acknowledges Getty Images as the primary image supplier for this title.

LET'S PLAY Basketball

CONTENTS

2   AV² Book Code
4   Getting Ready
6   What I Wear
8   What Else I Wear
10 What I Use
12 Where I Play
14 Playing the Game
16 More Game Play
18 Winning the Game
20 I Love Basketball
22 Basketball Facts
24 Word List

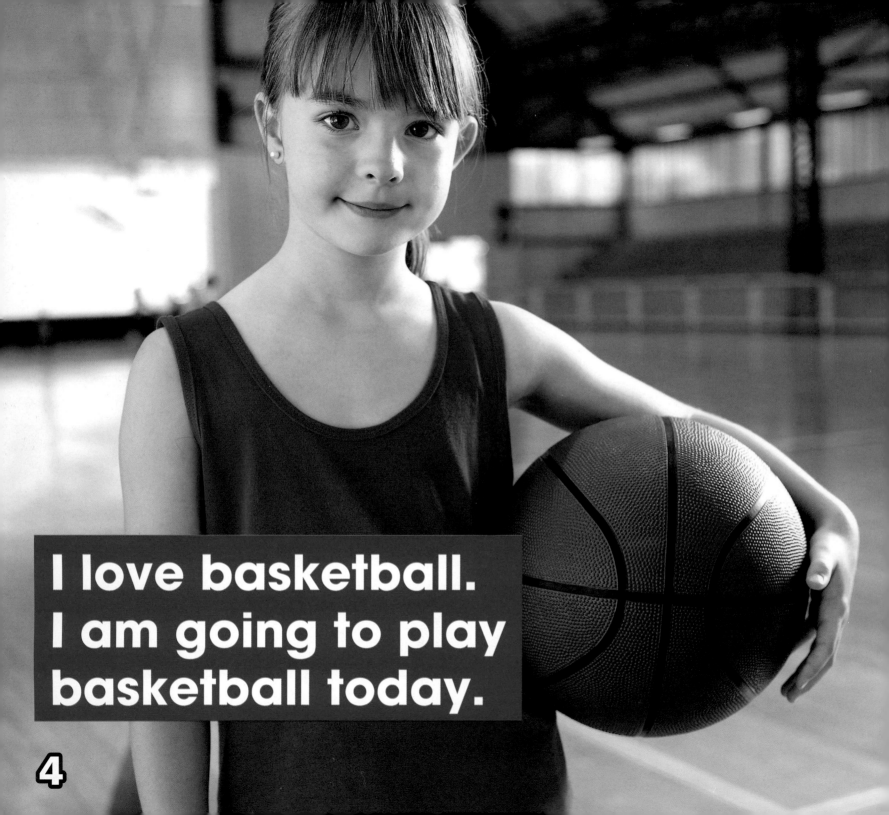

I love basketball.
I am going to play
basketball today.

4

Basketball was invented over 100 years ago.

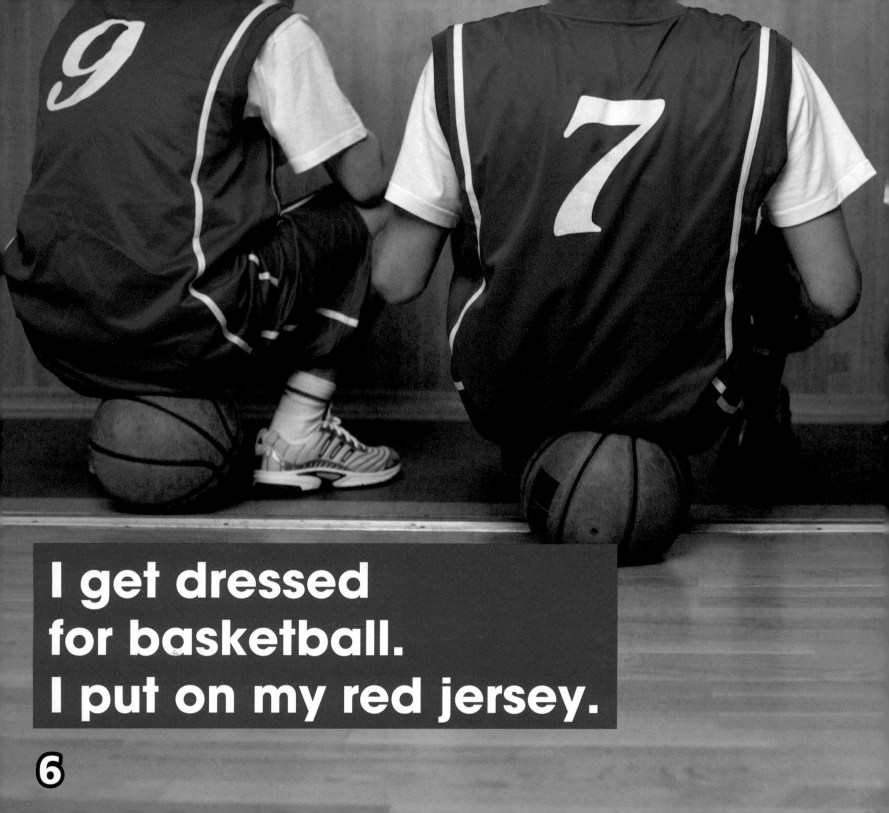

I get dressed
for basketball.
I put on my red jersey.

6

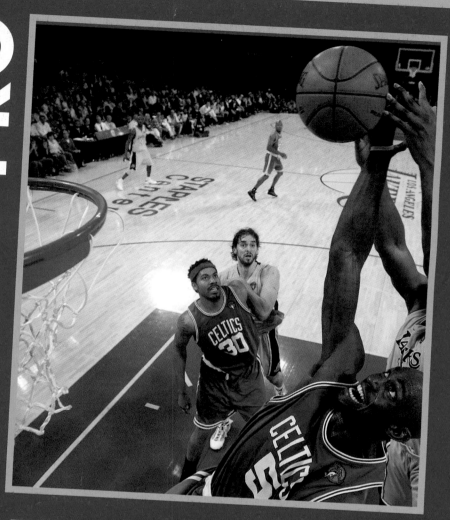

Players on a team wear the same color.

7

I put on shorts.
I put on shoes
with rubber bottoms.

Like a PRO

I get hot
when I play.
My clothes
help keep me cool.

9

I have a basketball.
It is round and orange.
It bounces.

10

Basketballs have a rubber bag inside.

I go to the
basketball court.
I meet my friends.
We are a team.

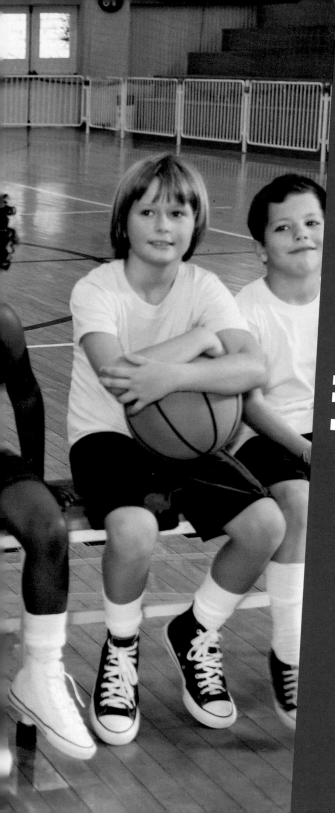

There are many lines and circles on the court.

The game starts.
I bounce the ball.
I pass the ball
to my team.

Bouncing a basketball while I move is called dribbling.

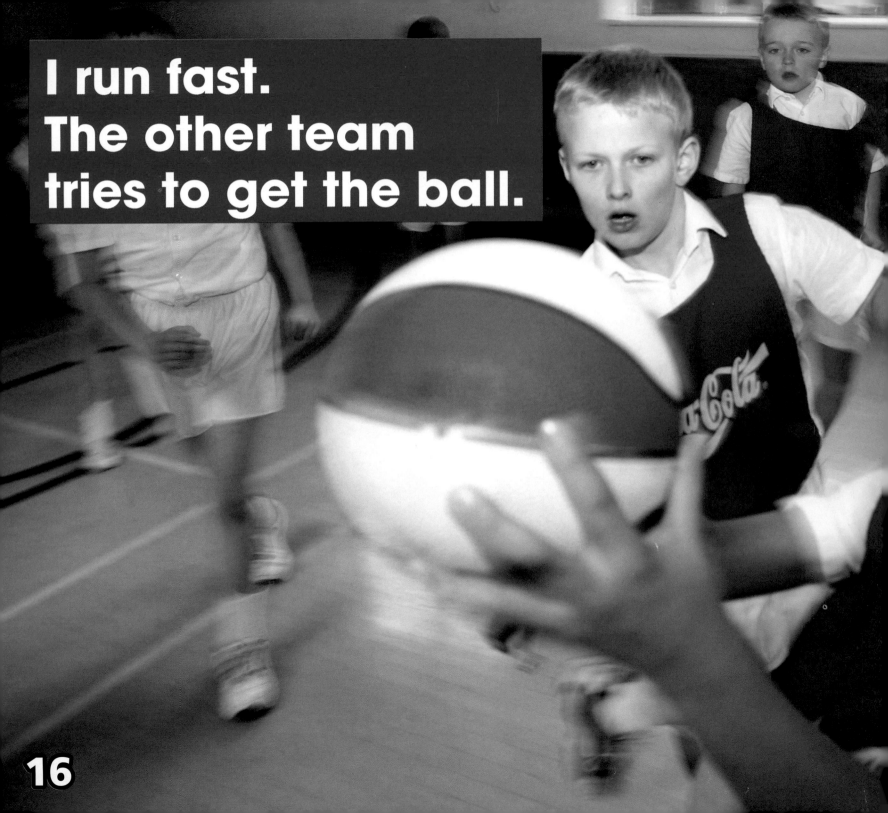

I run fast.
The other team
tries to get the ball.

16

I cannot bump or push other players to get the ball.

17

I shoot the ball at the basket. The ball goes in. My team cheers.

18

Some players
are very tall.
One of the
tallest is 7'6".

I love basketball.

BASKETBALL FACTS

This page provides more detail about the interesting facts found in the book.
Simply look at the corresponding page number to match the fact.

Pages 4-5

Basketball was invented in 1891 by a Canadian physical education teacher named Dr. James Naismith. The first games used peach baskets. Originally, basketballs had to be retrieved from the basket with a ladder each time a player scored. Later, open-ended nets were introduced.

Pages 6-7

Wearing the same color allows players to identify who is on their team at a glance. If two teams show up wearing the same colors, one team will put different colored shirts called pinnies over their jerseys so players can tell the difference between teams.

Pages 8-9

Basketball is a fast-paced game with lots of running. Sleeveless shirts and loose shorts allow for comfort and ease of movement. The most important piece of equipment for basketball players is shoes. They are light so players can run quickly, and the rubber bottoms prevent slipping on the wood floor.

Pages 10-11

Basketballs have a small valve in the side to pump air in if the ball gets too soft. The ball will not bounce very well unless it is full of air.

Pages 12–13

Lines on the floor show players where not to step outside the lines with the ball. The game begins in the center circle. Other lines show where players have to shoot from to get three points and where to line up for free throws.

Pages 14–15

The player with the ball has to dribble, pass, or shoot. Once the player touches the ball with both hands, he or she cannot continue dribbling. Players have 24 seconds to shoot at the basket, or they have to give the ball to the other team.

Pages 16–17

Basketball is not a contact sport. If a player knocks or pushes another player, he is given a foul. Referees may give the other team free throws at the basket or a throw-in at the sidelines, depending on where on the court the foul happened.

Pages 18–19

People of any height can play basketball. Professional teams often look for tall players because it gives them an advantage. Tall players have longer legs for jumping and longer arms for reaching the basket. One of the tallest players at 7'6" is Yao Ming. He plays for the Houston Rockets NBA team.

Pages 20–21

Playing a sport involves gear and a special place to play, and it also involves preparing the body to work hard. Eating healthy food helps fuel the body to do its best. Eating right makes bones stronger and gives muscles energy. A snack and drink after playing sports helps replace energy spent during a game.

23

WORD LIST

Research has shown that as much as 65 percent of all written material published in English is made up of 300 words. These 300 words cannot be taught using pictures or learned by sounding them out. They must be recognized by sight. This book contains 42 common sight words to help young readers improve their reading fluency and comprehension. This book also teaches young readers several important content words. These words are paired with pictures to aid in learning and improve understanding.

Page	Sight Words First Appearance	Page	Content Words First Appearance
4	I, play, to	4	basketball, today
5	over, was, years	5	years
6	for, get, on, my, put, red	6	jersey
7	a, same, the	7	color, players, team
8	with	8	bottoms, shoes, shorts, rubber
9	help, keep, me, when	9	clothes
10	and, have, is, it	11	bag
12	are, go, we	12	court, friends
13	lines, many, there	13	circles, lines
14	starts	14	ball, game
15	move, while	15	move
16	other, run	18	basket
17	or		
18	at, in		
19	of, one, some, very		

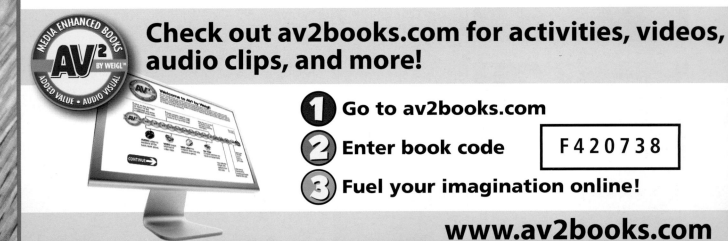

Check out av2books.com for activities, videos, audio clips, and more!

1 Go to av2books.com

2 Enter book code   F 4 2 0 7 3 8

3 Fuel your imagination online!

24

www.av2books.com